HISTORY'S
HEROES AND
VILLAINS
ADAM BOWETT
ILLUSTRATED BY CHRIS MOULD
Belitha Press

First published in Great Britain in 1995 by
Belitha Press Limited
31 Newington Green
London N16 9PU

ISBN 185561 314 X (Hardback)
ISBN 1 85561 359 X (Paperback)

Printed in China for Imago

British Library Cataloguing in Publication Data
CIP Data for this book is available from the British Library.
Editor: Carol Watson
Art Director: Frances McKay
Designer: Hayley Cove
Consultant: James Walvin

CONTENTS

INTRODUCTION

History would be very dull indeed without heroes and villains. In this book, you'll find plenty of both.

Some heroes, such as Florence Nightingale, set out to do heroic deeds. Others, such as Lawrence of Arabia and Claudius, became heroes reluctantly. The women of Weinsberg simply behaved with old-fashioned common sense, while Oskar Schindler combined humanity with good business to save thousands of lives.

Then there are the villains. Some, such as Blackbeard, are bad through and through. There are no excuses either for Al Capone. But what are we to make of Herod, a once sensible king who went mad in his old age? Vlad Tepes, known as Dracula, was both hero and villain. Like Genghis Khan he was a brave man, with some very nasty habits. And as for poor Mata Hari – she wanted a life of excitement, but in the end she probably wished she'd stayed at home.

Words in **bold** in the text are explained in the glossary on page 31.

BLACKBEARD

Captain Edward Teach was born in the late 17th century. Early in the 18th century he fought for the English as a **privateer** in the Caribbean. When the war ended in 1713, Teach began his career as a pirate, and became known as Blackbeard.

Blackbeard was a fearsome-looking pirate. His thick, black beard reached down to his chest and his long hair was plaited and twisted up around his ears. Blackbeard brandished a musket and cutlass, carried six pistols strapped across his body and was strong, cunning and totally fearless.

Blackbeard's favourite trick

Blackbeard went into battle with lighted tapers flaming in his beard, so that his face was wreathed in billowing smoke.

Blackbeard and his pirate crew attacked and plundered ships all over the Atlantic and Caribbean, and soon he became known for his great daring and cruelty. Even his own men were afraid of him. Once, Blackbeard shut himself and his crew in the hold of their ship and lit pots of **brimstone.** He roared with laughter as his men staggered about, coughing and choking in the poisonous fumes.

Another time, while drinking and playing cards with two crewmen, Blackbeard suddenly blew out the candles, drew out two pistols and fired them under the table. In the darkness, one of his men, Israel Hands, was shot in the knee and maimed for life.

After two years at sea, Blackbeard's luck ran out. A British naval **sloop** chased his ship and it ran aground. Defiantly, the pirates boarded the enemy ship and did battle with the navy.

The commander of the sloop, Robert Maynard, fought a ferocious duel with Blackbeard. Finally, with 25 separate wounds, the pirate collapsed and died.

Oskar Schindler

During the Second World War, Jews all over Europe were persecuted by the Nazis of Germany. Brainwashed by their leader, Adolf Hitler, the Nazis mistakenly believed that the Jews were fit only for slave labour or worse. In Poland the Nazis were particularly cruel. At first, in the cities of Warsaw, Lodz and Cracow, the Jews were made to live in **ghettos.** But after 1942, the Nazis forced all the Jews to live in **concentration camps.** There, they were shot, gassed or worked to death.

In 1939, Oskar Schindler, a German businessman, arrived in Cracow. Oskar was shocked when he saw the way the Nazis treated the Jews. He had just bought a factory and decided to recruit Jews to work there. At first, the Nazis spared Jews who produced goods or weapons useful to Germany, so by giving them jobs, Schindler prevented some Jews from being sent to the concentration camps.

Although life was not easy for Oskar's Jews, they knew that as long as they worked for him they were safe. For four years, Schindler kept his factory going saving more and more Jews from certain death.

By 1944, the Nazis had to retreat from Poland. Oskar's factory in Cracow was closed and his Jewish workers were sent to the camps.

When he heard that his Jews faced the gas chambers, Schindler knew he had to act fast. He set up another factory in Czechoslavakia. By paying the Nazis large amounts of money, he persuaded them to let him transport his Jewish workers there. Oskar Schindler took 1,200 Jews to his new factory. There they worked in safety until the war ended in May 1945.

A hero's grave

After the war, the Jews did not forget Oskar. When Schindler died in 1947 he was buried in Jerusalem. A plaque in his honour was placed in the Park of Heroes, in Tel Aviv.

Herod the Great was born in 73 BC in southern Palestine. Ten years later, the Romans invaded and occupied the land. As Herod grew up, he decided that the only way to a successful future was to impress the Romans with his talents. And this he did. So, eventually, in 47 BC he was appointed Governor of Galilee, and seven years later, the Emperor Augustus made him King of **Judea**.

Herod was called 'great' because, in some ways, he achieved great things during his reign. He improved the way the country was governed and built ports, cities and fortresses to please the Romans.

Unfortunately, as well as being an able and clever king, Herod was crafty, suspicious and cruel. He was so worried about threats to his kingdom that he thought that everyone was plotting against him.

One day, in a fit of jealous rage, Herod murdered his wife, her mother, and the high priest. Some years later, he executed his own son, and the sons of his sister, Salome. The older he grew, the worse Herod became.

Shortly before his death, Herod heard rumours that a future king was to be born in Judea. His advisers told him that, according to the scriptures, the new king of the Jews would be born in the town of Bethlehem, near Jerusalem.

Although he was old and frail, Herod could not bear the idea of a rival. So he ordered his advisers to search for the baby that was to be the new Jewish king. When they failed to find the child, Herod flew into a rage. He ordered his soldiers to kill every boy in Bethlehem under the age of two. This terrible deed became known as the Massacre of the Innocents.

Jesus of Nazareth

The baby described in the scriptures was called Jesus. His parents, Mary and Joseph, were warned by God of Herod's anger and fled secretly to Egypt with their child.

THE LADY OF THE LAMP

Florence Nightingale was born in Florence, Italy. In 1837, at the age of 17, she felt that God was telling her that she had a mission. Florence had always wanted to be a nurse, and thought that she was being called to care for the sick and dying. Her wealthy parents had hoped that Florence would marry a rich husband, and were horrified by their daughter's interest in medicine.

Despite all opposition, however, at the age of 30, Florence went to Germany to train as a nurse.

When the Crimean War broke out in 1854, Florence found her mission. The British Secretary of State for War asked her to take charge of the British Military Hospital at Scutari, in Turkey.

The conditions in the Turkish hospital were appalling. There was disease and dirt everywhere, water was rationed and the food was inedible. Rats, fleas and lice swarmed over the wounded, who lay in corridors as there was a shortage of beds.

Florence reorganized the hospital and worked 20 hours a day, supervising the 5,000 soldiers in her care. Every night, holding a lamp to light her way, she visited the wards to check on her patients. The soldiers loved her, and soon Florence became known as the 'lady of the lamp'.

Stories of Florence's devotion to the sick were published in the newspapers at home. When the war ended and Florence returned to England, she refused all the honours offered her and spent the rest of her life nursing.

Mystery illness

In 1857 Florence became ill. She was an invalid until her death in 1910, although no cause for her illness was found. Throughout this time she devoted her life to training nurses, and in 1860 founded the Nightingale School for Nurses at St Thomas' Hospital, London.

Scrubbers

One of the first things Florence did was to order 200 scrubbing brushes, and she and her nurses cleaned the hospital from top to bottom.

AL CAPONE

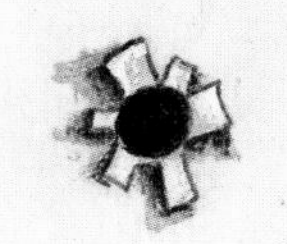

Alphonse Capone is probably the most famous gangster of all time. He was born in New York in 1899, the son of poor Italian **immigrants.** Al's life of crime began when he was young. In one youthful scrape, his face was slashed with a razor, leaving a terrible scar. From then on he was given the nickname, Scarface.

When he was 20, Al moved to Chicago, a well-known centre for criminal gangs. They organized illegal gambling and drinking, and money-making schemes called **rackets**. Al Capone and an old pal from New York, Johnny Torrio, set up together, and they soon became very powerful in the criminal world.

In 1920, the US government banned the sale of all alcohol. This was an opportunity for many gangsters to make huge fortunes **bootlegging** illegal alcohol.

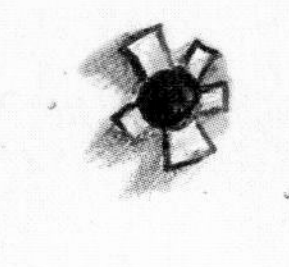

At this point Al Capone's career took off. Soon he was the most powerful man in the Chicago underworld.

On 14 February 1929, Al Capone's gang wiped out the gang of Bugsy Morant in the St Valentine's Day Massacre. After this mass murder, Al controlled nearly all the rackets in Chicago.

Despite his reputation for violence, theft and murder, Al Capone was never convicted of his crimes. His victims were either dead or too terrified to give evidence against him. Al bribed policemen, lawyers and judges to make sure that he never went to jail.

In 1931, Al Capone was finally arrested for not paying taxes. He was found guilty, fined $80,000 and sent to prison for 11 years. There Al became very ill, and so he was released from jail. He died before he was 50.

The Chicago piano

One of the gangsters' weapons was the Thompson sub-machine gun. This became known as the Chicago piano because the gangsters liked the 'tunes', or noise it made as they fired.

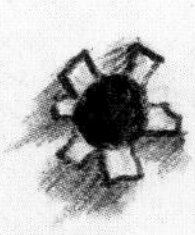

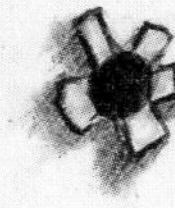

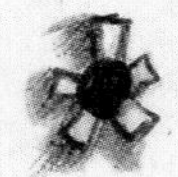

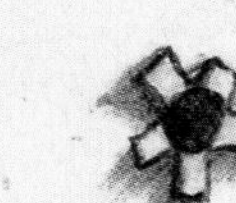

Emperor Claudius

Claudius was born in Lyons, France, in 10 BC. His full name was Tiberius Claudius Drusus Nero Germanicus, but not surprisingly he was called Claudius for short. His mother was a Roman noblewoman and his father a famous general. Claudius' uncle was the Emperor Tiberius, whose son Caligula later became emperor.

No one imagined for a moment that, one day, Claudius would rule the Roman Empire. Claudius was unattractive, clumsy, coarse-mannered and often ill. He also had a stammer and a limp. In fact, he was an embarrassment to his relatives.

To keep Claudius out of the way, his family employed a famous historian called Livy to teach him history, grammar and Greek. Claudius was a good scholar, and shut up in his library he was content. Nobody bothered him, and he could escape from the politics of palace life.

Unlucky in love

Claudius did not make a success of marriage. He had four wives in all. He divorced two and executed one. Finally, in 54 AD, his fourth wife poisoned him.

In 37 AD Claudius' cousin Caligula became emperor. He was cruel and more than a little mad. So no one was surprised when one day Caligula was murdered. The guards immediately searched the palace for his murderer. They found Claudius hiding, terrified, behind a curtain. Luckily for Claudius the guards were in a good mood, so instead of killing him, they made him emperor in Caligula's place.

Claudius turned out to be a good emperor. He was fair and wise and improved Roman politics and law. And to show he wasn't as feeble as he looked, Claudius invaded a few countries too.

MATA HARI

Mata Hari was born in 1876, in Holland. Her real name was Margaretha Geertruida Zelle. Margaretha was tall and beautiful, and at the age of 18 she attracted the attentions of dashing Captain Campbell Macleod. After a whirlwind romance, they were married.

Macleod became an officer in the Dutch colonial army. In 1897, he was posted to the Far East, and for the next few years he and Margaretha lived in Java. Here she observed the exotic women dancers of the East. Margaretha found army life very dull, and bored by everything, she finally left her husband.

Margaretha decided that it would be much more exciting to be a dancer in Paris. She gave herself the stage name of Mata Hari and began to perform the exotic dances she remembered from her time in Java.

Mata Hari was an amazing success. The men of Paris flocked to see her show, and there was always a queue of admirers outside her dressing-room door.

When, in 1914, the First World War broke out, Mata Hari added a sideline to her act. She travelled round the major cities of Europe, and coaxed vital military secrets from her lovestruck admirers. The trouble was, nobody really knew whose side she was on. She told the French she was spying on the Germans, and she told the Germans she was spying on the French.

In 1916, Mata Hari had secret meetings with the German consul in Holland. But the French authorities found out and in 1917 she was arrested in Paris.

Mata Hari was put on trial in a military court. This time her beauty and charm failed her and she was found guilty of **espionage.** On 15 October 1917, Mata Hari was shot by a French firing squad.

Guilty or not?

No one really knows whether or not Mata Hari did spy against France. Certainly, she was a dangerous woman, but chiefly, as it turned out, to herself.

LAWRENCE OF ARABIA

Thomas Edward Lawrence was the son of an Irish landowner. He wanted to be an archaeologist, so after he graduated from Oxford University, he spent three years in Iraq, excavating the ruins of an ancient town called Carchemish. There, he learned Arabic, wore Arab clothes and ate Arab food.

In 1914, the First World War broke out and so Lawrence joined the British Army. Lieutenant Lawrence was sent first to Cairo, where his knowledge of Arabic and experience of the Middle East made him an ideal **intelligence officer**. Lawrence had become friends with the Arab leader, King Feisal. Together, the two planned to drive the Turks from Arabia.

Lawrence abandoned his British Army uniform and wore instead the flowing robes and headdress of the desert Arabs. Riding a camel, he led dashing raids on the Turks, blowing up railway lines and attacking convoys.

In July 1917, Lawrence and Feisal had their biggest success when the Arabs captured the port of Aquaba on the Red Sea. A year later, the Arab army rode triumphantly into Damascus, the capital of Syria, and the desert war was over.

By the end of the First World War, Lawrence had reached the rank of Lieutenant-Colonel. He became a celebrity and was given the nickname Lawrence of Arabia. But he was not interested in fame. He refused all honours, and resigned his commission. Later, he joined the army as a private under a false name, and went on to work in the air force as a mechanic.

Tragic death

One day, as Lawrence rode his motorbike along a quiet road in Dorset, he met two boys on bicycles. Swerving to avoid them, Lawrence crashed his bike and was killed. The man who had survived so many dangers in war died in an English country lane.

VLAD THE IMPALER

To the people of Rumania, Vlad Tepes (also known as 'the Impaler') is a national hero. The rest of us know him as the villainous, mythical character, Count Dracula, the ghastly vampire who survived by drinking the blood of his victims. But who was the real Dracula?

Between 1456 and 1462, Vlad Tepes was the ruler of Wallachia, a province of Rumania. He gained the throne by killing the previous king. Anyone who opposed him was ruthlessly eliminated, and Vlad became known for his cruelty.

Vlad saved his greatest atrocities for the Turks. At this time the Turkish Empire of Sultan Mehmed II stretched into Europe. Vlad was not going to be dictated to by a Turkish sultan and he refused to pay the yearly tax of 10,000 ducats due to the powerful emperor. He crossed the River Danube with his soldiers and attacked the Turks at every opportunity.

In 1461, in a campaign against the Turks, Vlad's lust for blood grew. He and his soldiers wiped out the inhabitants of an entire valley and impaled more than 23,000 people on sharp, wooden stakes. The sultan wept when he heard of this terrible bloodshed.

Later that year, the sultan sent two ambassadors to discuss peace with Vlad. But Vlad did not trust the Turks. So, in a surprise attack, he captured the ambassadors, and impaled both men and their entire retinue.

In 1462, Vlad was imprisoned in Hungary. He was released 12 years later and was killed in 1477, three years after his release. Without Vlad to defend it, Wallachia soon fell to the Turks, and was part of their empire until the 18th century.

Dracula – the myth

The story of Dracula the Vampire began in 1809, when a German historian called JC von Engel wrote about Vlad's bloody deeds. Years later, the English author, Bram Stoker combined Engel's history with Rumanian legends to create *Dracula*, one of the most famous horror novels ever written.

MAHATMA GANDHI

Mahatma Gandhi was born in 1869 at Porbandar, in western India. When he was 18 he went to England to study law. Gandhi was lonely in London, but he stayed long enough to finish his studies. He then returned to India where he struggled to make a living. Then he took a job representing a firm of Indian merchants in a court case in South Africa. What he saw there changed the course of his life.

Gandhi was shocked at the way the British treated non-Europeans in South Africa, because of the colour of their skin. Gandhi was banned from hotels, and thrown out of a first-class railway carriage. He could not believe this intolerant attitude was right. He decided to dedicate his life to fighting racial prejudice. During his 21 years in South Africa, Gandhi gradually became a confident political leader.

In 1914, Gandhi returned to India. By now he was convinced that the people of his country must oppose British rule. But Gandhi was not a violent man. He believed that the best way to bring about change was through discussion and peaceful protest. Soon millions of Indians supported Gandhi in his opposition to their British overlords.

One of Gandhi's most successful campaigns was a mass protest against paying a tax on salt. 'Salt is owned by no one,' said Gandhi. 'It should be free to all.' To show their disapproval and disobedience, he led thousands of Indians on a 400 kilometre walk to the sea. More than 60,000 people were imprisoned, including Gandhi himself, but still the British were unable to stop the protest.

In 1947, India finally became independent of the British. But Gandhi's struggle was not yet over. Once the British had left the country, fighting broke out among the Indians. Muslims and Hindus fought for control of the new Indian state. Gandhi's efforts to unite the two religious groups were in vain, and on 30 January 1948 he was assassinated by a fanatic. The great man of peace died a violent death.

The great soul

Gandhi's real name was Mohandas Karamchand Gandhi, but the Indians called him Mahatma, which means 'the great soul'.

Genghis Khan

Few names in history have inspired such fear as that of Genghis Khan. Some stories say that he was born holding a clot of blood in his hand.

Genghis Khan was born around AD 1160 in Mongolia. His people were nomads who wandered over the barren desert lands of Central Asia. Genghis' father was chief of his tribe and called his son Temujin.

As was the tribal custom, Temujin married at the age of nine. But then his father was poisoned by an enemy clan called the Tartars. As Temujin was not old enough to lead his tribe, they abandoned the boy, and he and his family struggled to stay alive.

So Temujin learned at an early age that he had to be strong, ruthless and more cunning than his enemies in order to survive.

When he grew up, Temujin began to unite all the Mongol clans under his command. Anyone who refused to join him was hunted down and killed.

In 1206, Temujin and his warriors defeated the Tartars in battle. To avenge his father, and avoid all threat to his power, Temujin ordered his soldiers to kill every Tartar man who was taller than a cart axle. Only the children survived.

Temujin called himself Genghis Khan, which means 'universal ruler' and prepared the entire Mongol nation for war. Every man was trained to be a superb horseman and expert archer. His warriors moved swiftly, travelling day and night and living off the land.

The armies of Genghis Khan were so savage and terrible that few armies could withstand them. In 1211, the Mongols invaded China, and by 1215 they had captured the capital, Beijing.

After this, Genghis attacked Persia. Although the Persians fought bravely, their cities were captured and the people were slaughtered. So whenever anyone heard that the troops of Genghis Khan were approaching, they were filled with despair and surrendered.

Violent to the end

Even after he died, Genghis Khan caused great slaughter. His death had to be kept a secret until his son, Ogodei was proclaimed his successor. So as they carried his coffin, the members of his funeral party killed anyone they met on the way.

THE WOMEN OF WEINSBERG

In 1140, King Konrad of Germany decided to invade a small town in Bavaria called Weinsberg. The leader of the townsfolk, Wolf of Bavaria, gathered his men and repeatedly beat off the king's assaults. But eventually King Konrad captured the town, and by this time he was in a furious temper. 'You will pay for your defiance!' he boomed. 'All the women must leave, and all the men will be hanged.'

This was a terrible sentence. Many of the women refused to leave. Others begged the king to be merciful. But King Konrad was in no mood to compromise. He ordered the women to leave Weinsberg in the morning and to take only what they could carry on their backs.

That evening, the women of Weinsberg packed up their belongings. Suddenly, one of them had an idea. 'Didn't the king say we could take with us whatever we can carry on our backs?' she said. 'In that case, I will carry my husband, since I value him more than anything in the world.'

The next morning a strange sight greeted the king's guards at the town gate. The women of Weinsberg were queueing to leave, each with her husband on her back. King Konrad was quickly sent for. He took one look at the scene and knew he was beaten.

'A king cannot go back on his word,' he declared. 'These brave women are devoted to their husbands, and they are lucky men to have such wives.' Then he pardoned both the wives and the husbands. 'You may all stay in Weinsberg,' he said, 'and live together in peace.'

A proverbial story

The story of the women of Weinsberg is remembered in Germany to this day and 'loyal as the women of Weinsberg' is a famous saying.

TIME LINE

Period	Dates	Person
100 BC	73 BC – 4 BC	Herod
BC	10 BC – AD 54	Emperor Claudius
Birth of Christ		
1000 AD		
1100	1140	The Women of Weinsberg
1200	c 1162 – 1227	Genghis Khan
1400	c 1430 – 1477	Vlad the Impaler
1600 – 1700	c 1680 – 1715	Blackbeard
1800 – 1900	1820 – 1910	Florence Nightingale
	1876 – 1917	Mata Hari
	1888 – 1935	T. E. Lawrence
	1869 – 1948	Mahatma Gandhi
	1899 – 1947	Al Capone
	1908 – 1974	Oskar Schindler